Vistas, American West

By Melvin Morales

Vistas, American West

Copyright © 2024 by CV Management Solutions, LLC

All photographs and content in this photo book are the sole creation and property of CV Management Solutions, LLC. These images are protected under copyright law and may not be reproduced, distributed, or transmitted in any form or by any means, including photocopying, recording, or other electronic or mechanical methods, without the prior written permission of the photographer and/or publisher, except in the case of brief quotations embodied in critical reviews and certain other noncommercial uses permitted by copyright law.

For permission requests or inquiries, please contact:

CV Management Solutions LLC
30 N GOULD STREET SUITE R
SHERIDAN, WY 82801

ISBN: 9798321605882

Printed in United States

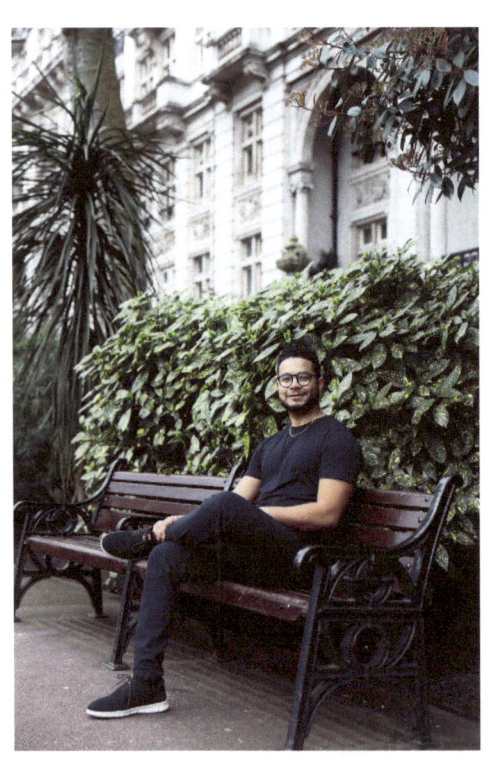

Welcome to Vistas, American West – a photography book born from a passion for adventure, exploration, and the art of capturing moments frozen in time.

Born in Puerto Rico and raised in Rhode Island, my journey began with a relentless sense of curiosity and a desire to explore the beauty of the world firsthand. It was during my high school years that I discovered my love for photography, initially through the lens of my iPhone 5, before graduating to my first Nikon camera. The idea of capturing moments in time captivated me.

Venturing to Boston for college, where I pursued studies in Industrial Design at Wentworth Institute of Technology, I found myself immersed in the vibrant tapestry of urban life. It was here that I honed my craft, experimenting with various genres from street to portrait photography, always seeking new perspectives and angles to capture the essence of the moment. Eventually, my journey led me to discover the balance and beauty inherently in landscape photography as I would escape the city limits to find peace.

Leaving behind the familiar sights of New England, I embarked on a journey westward, driven by new opportunities and a desire to witness the breathtaking vistas that the American West had to offer. From the soaring mountains of the Rocky Mountains to the sweeping deserts of the Southwest, each landscape told a story of unparalleled beauty and grandeur.

This book is a culmination of places across the Western states, a visual homage to the majesty of the American West. Captured during road trips spanning eight western states, these images serve as a testament to exploration and the pursuit of adventure in life.

Never Settle & Keep Exploring

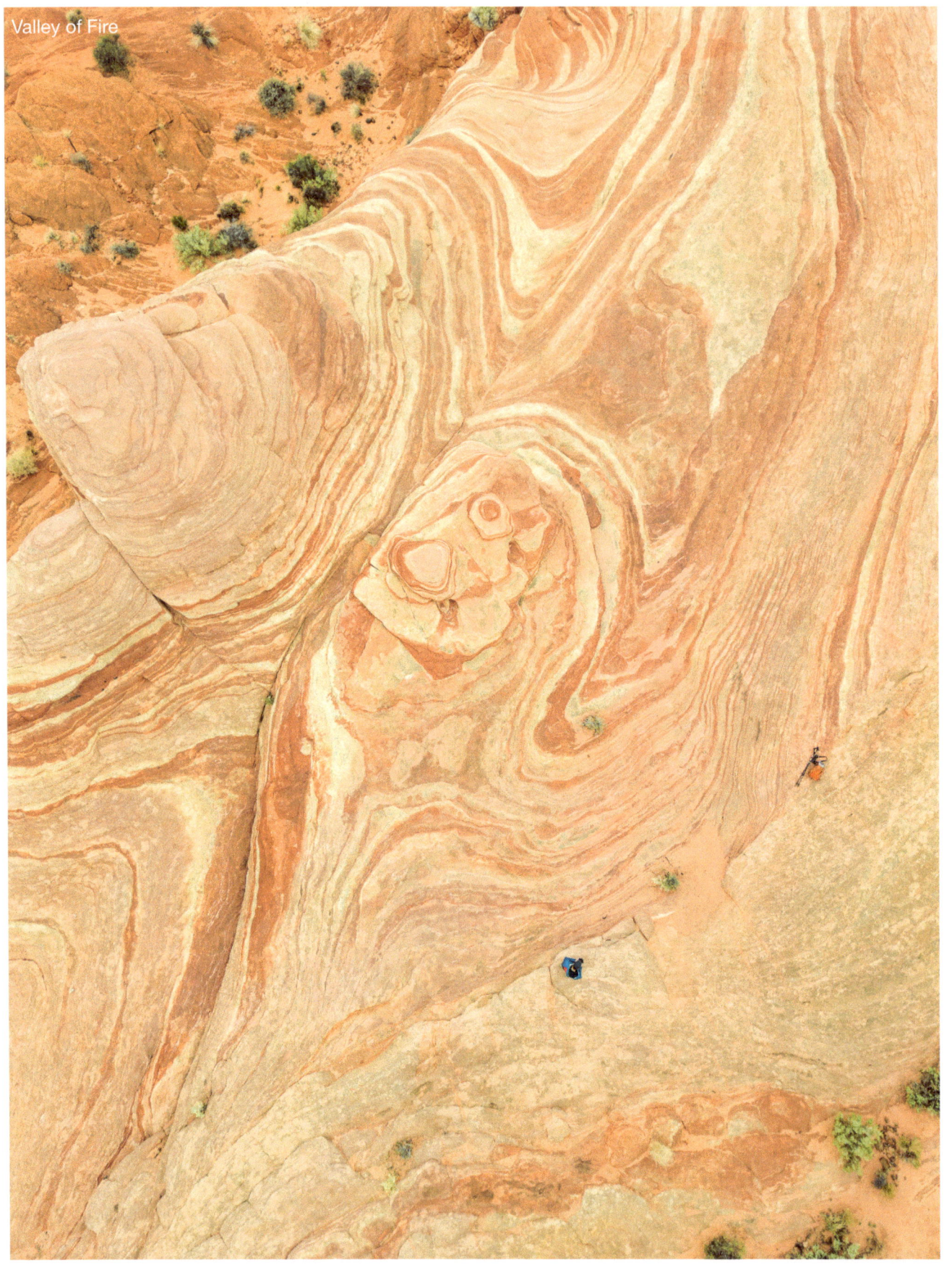
Valley of Fire

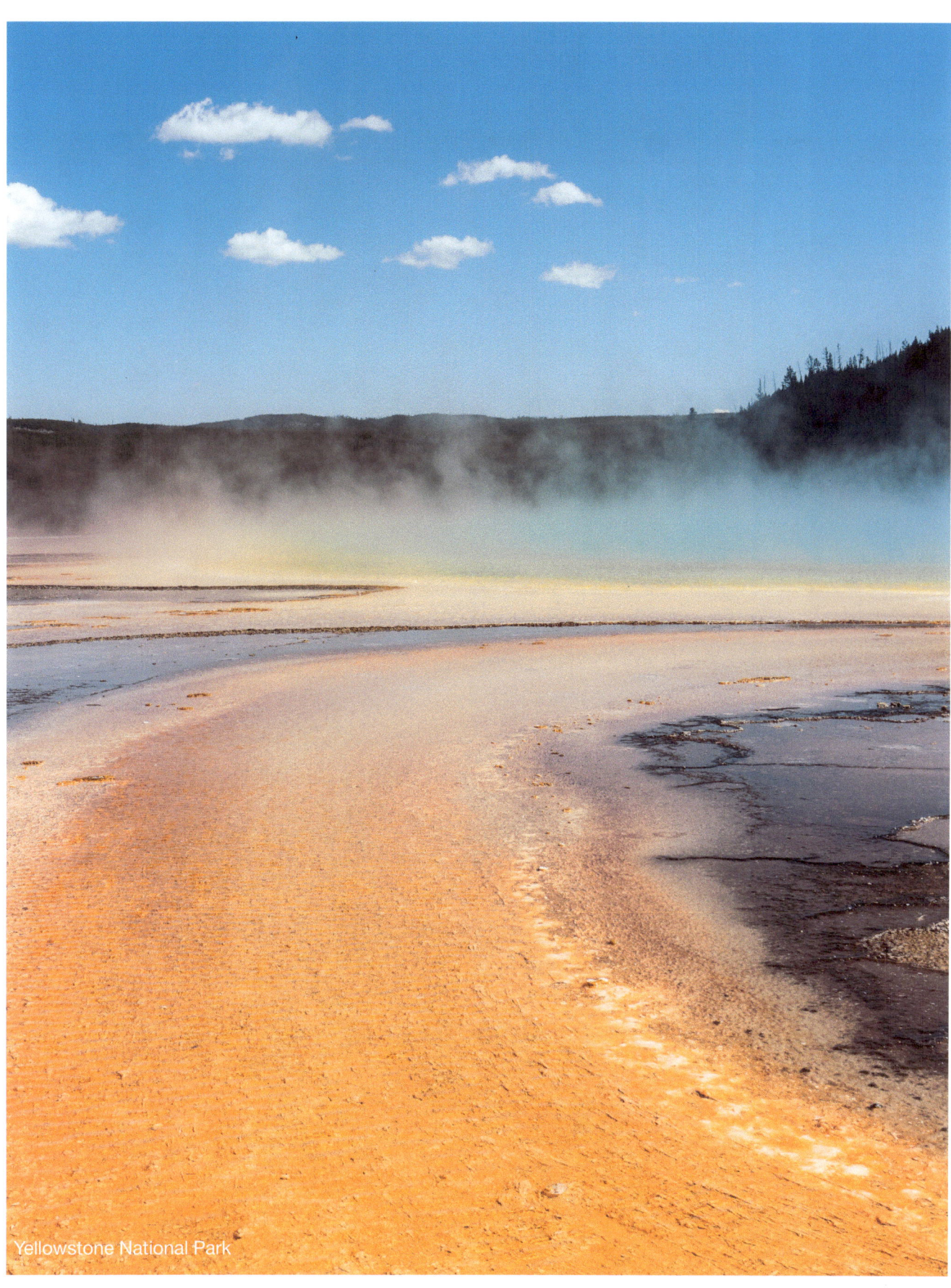

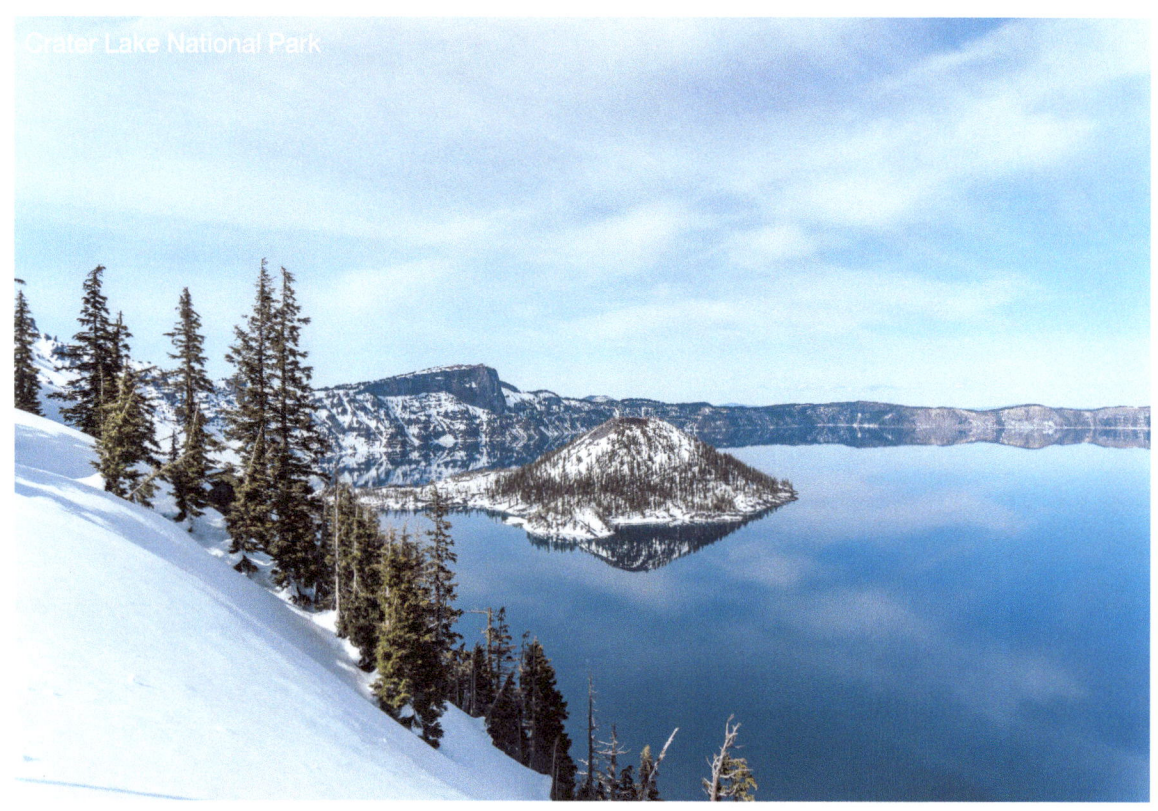

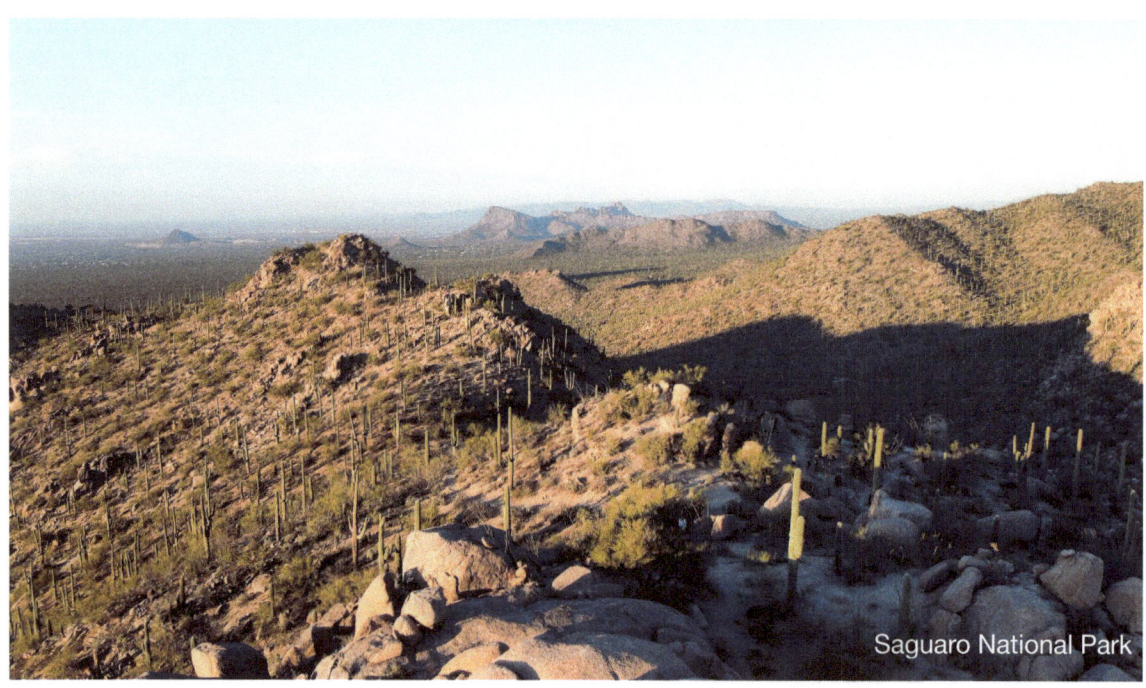

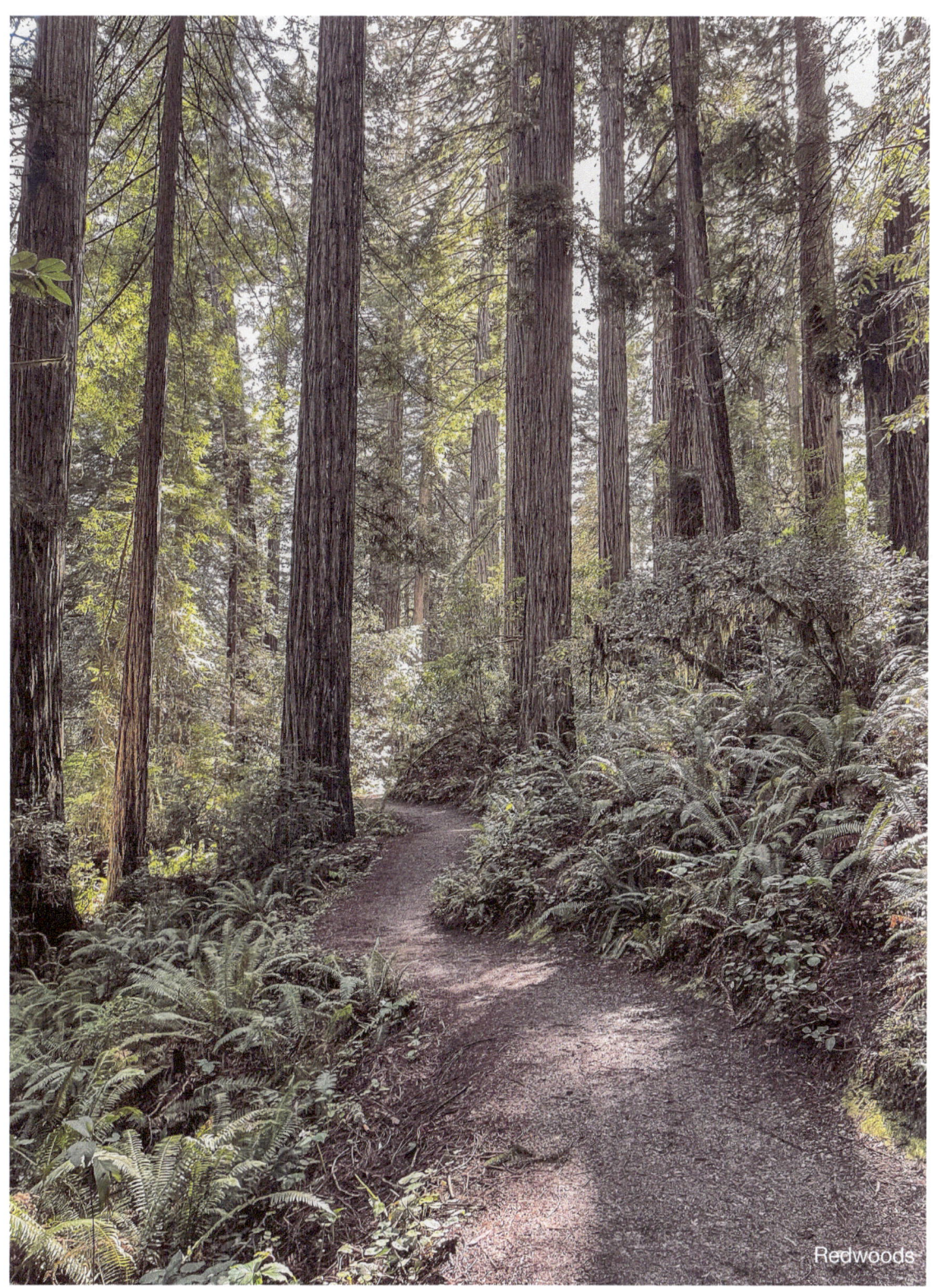

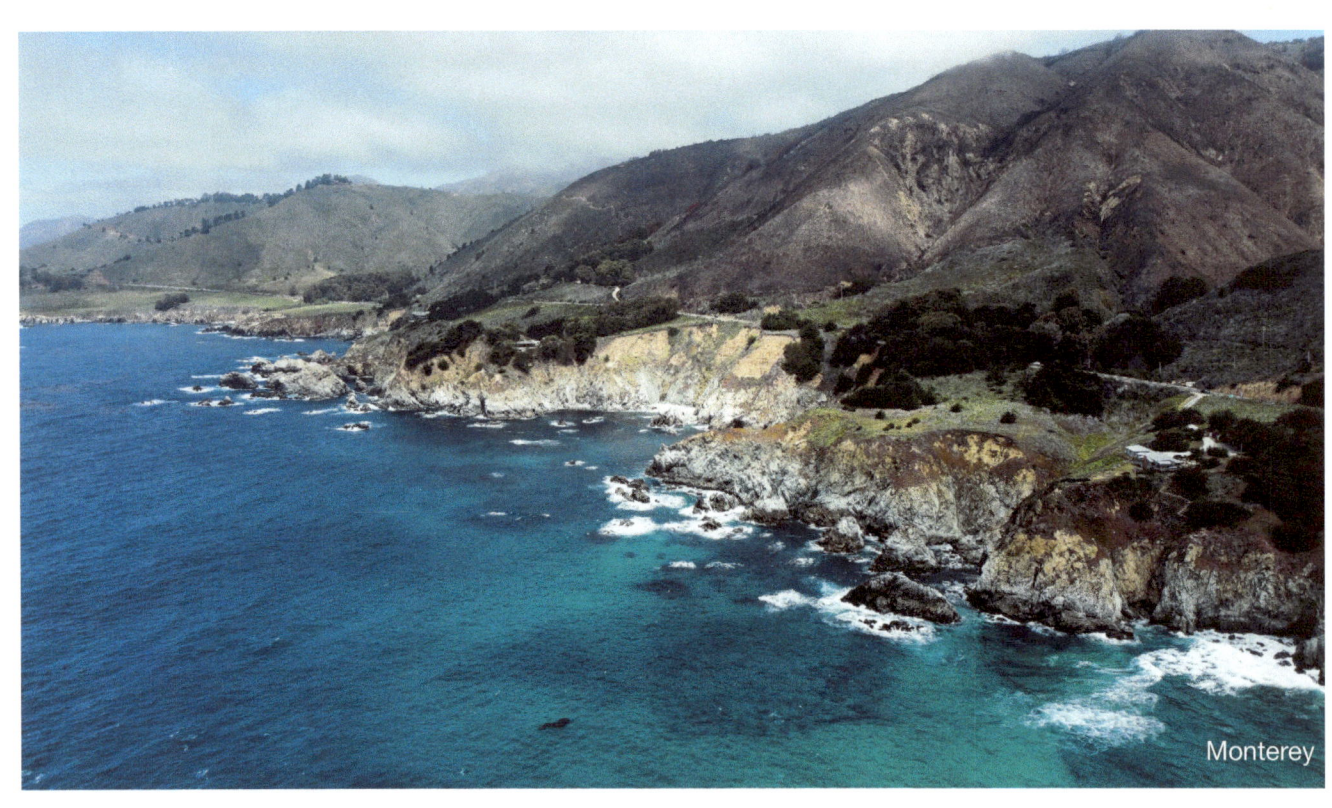

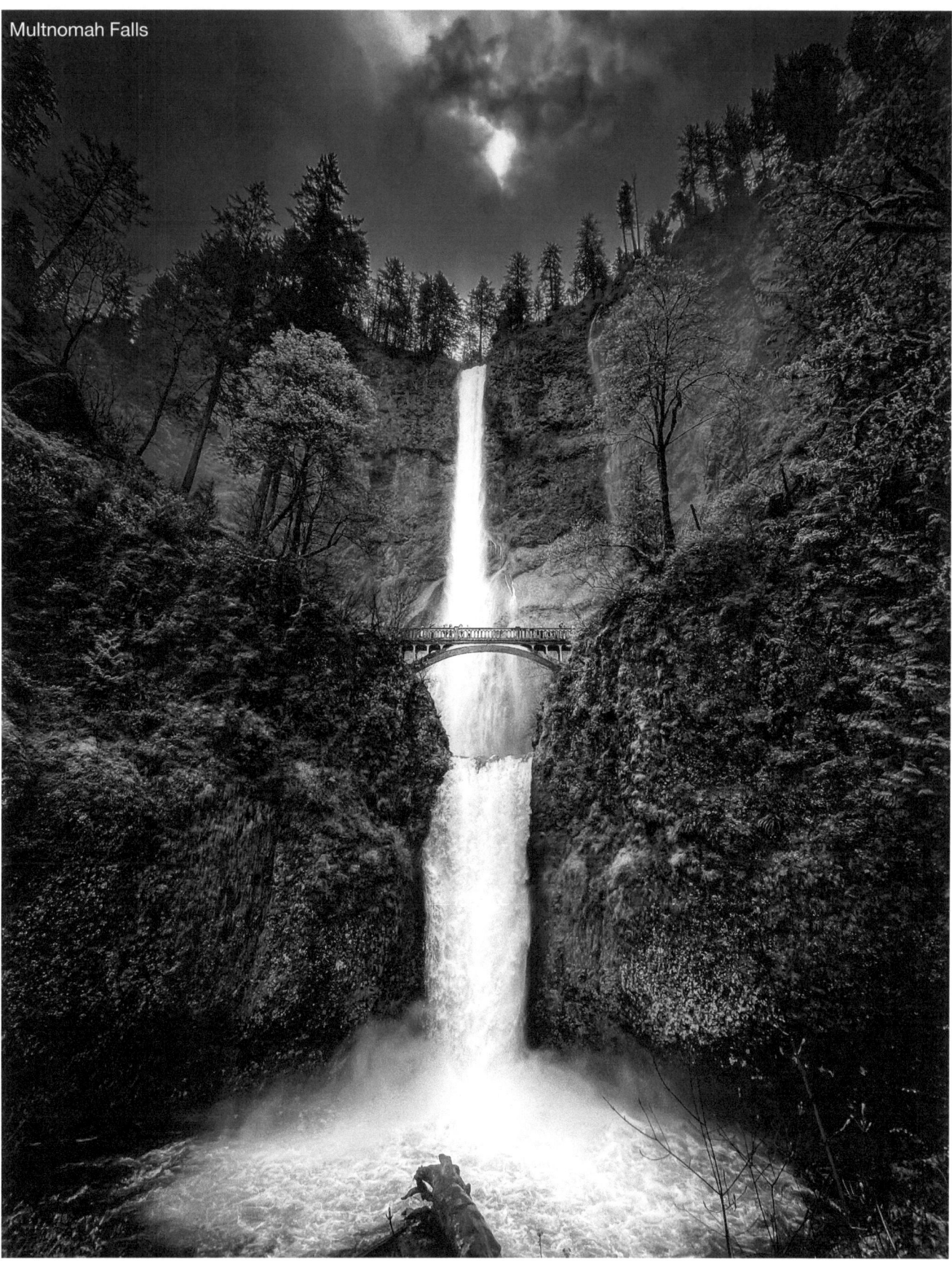

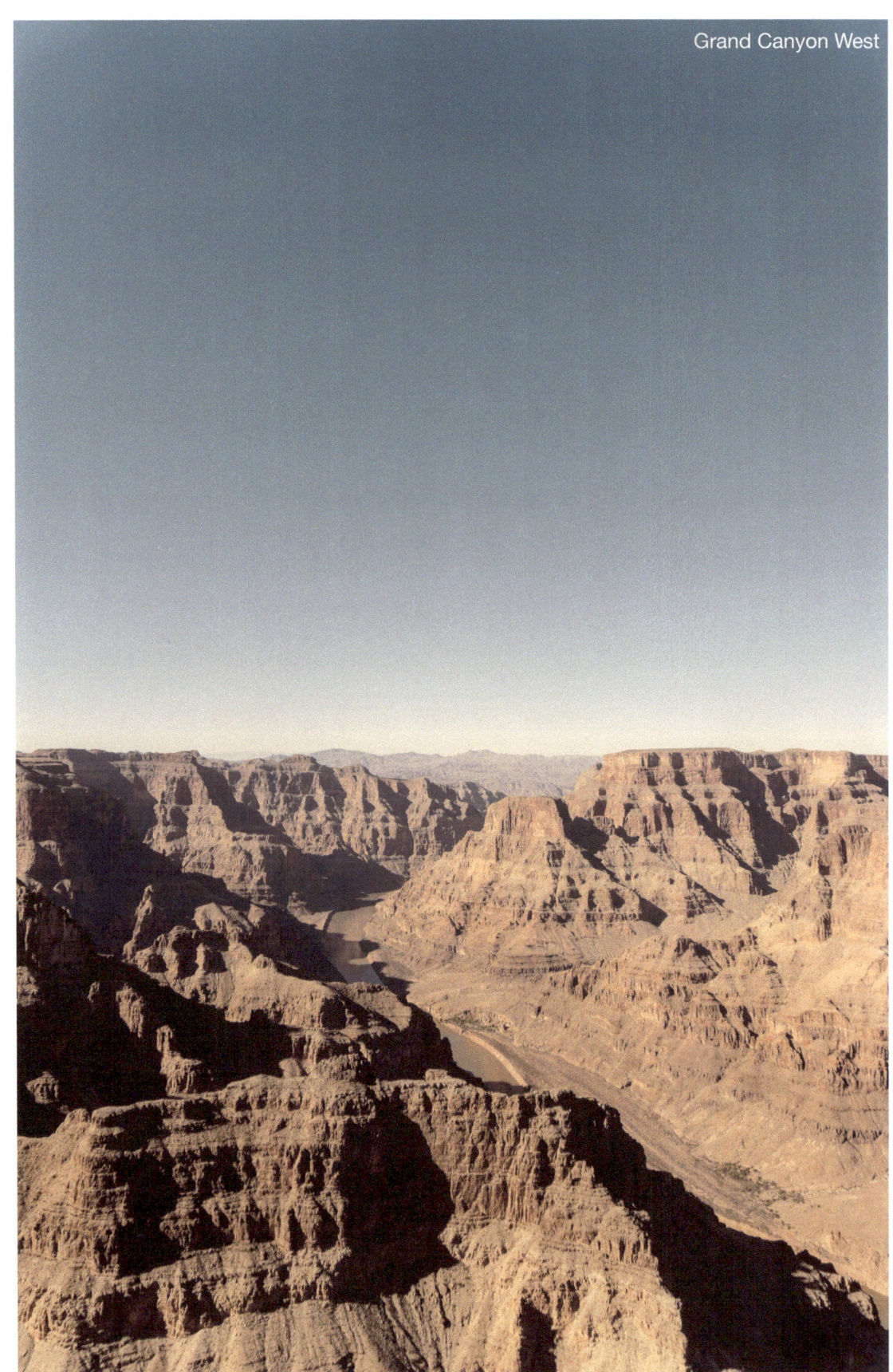

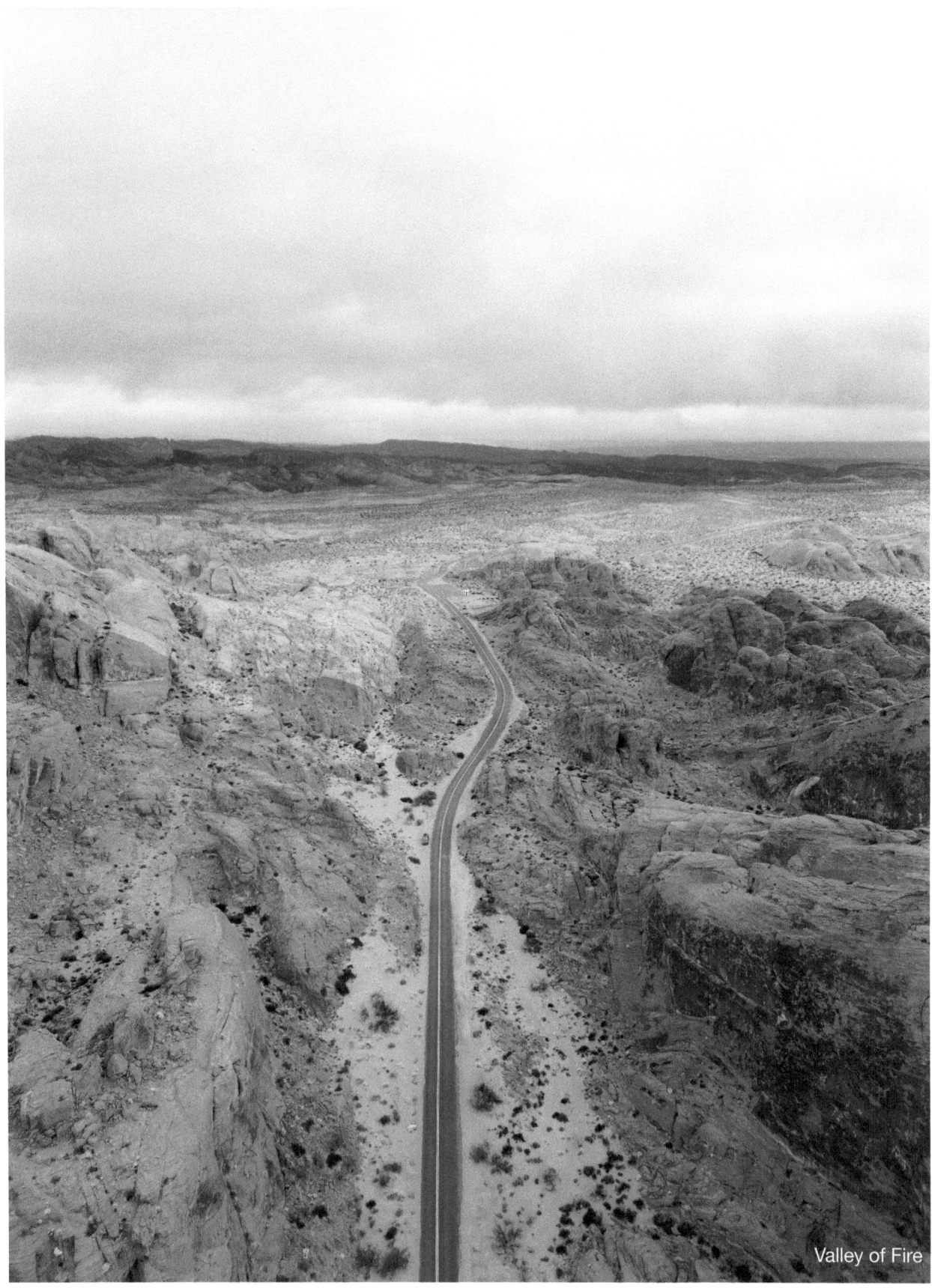

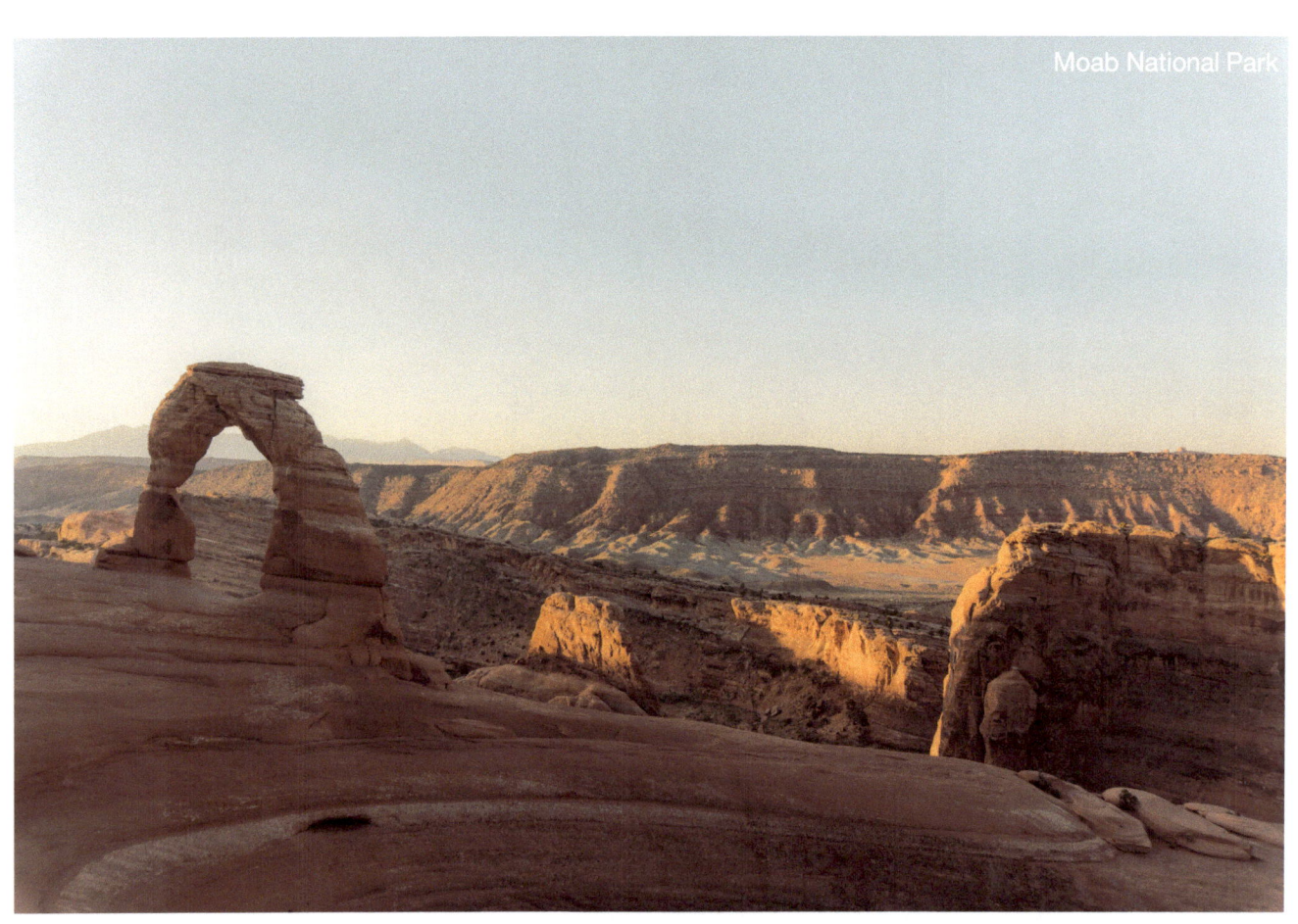

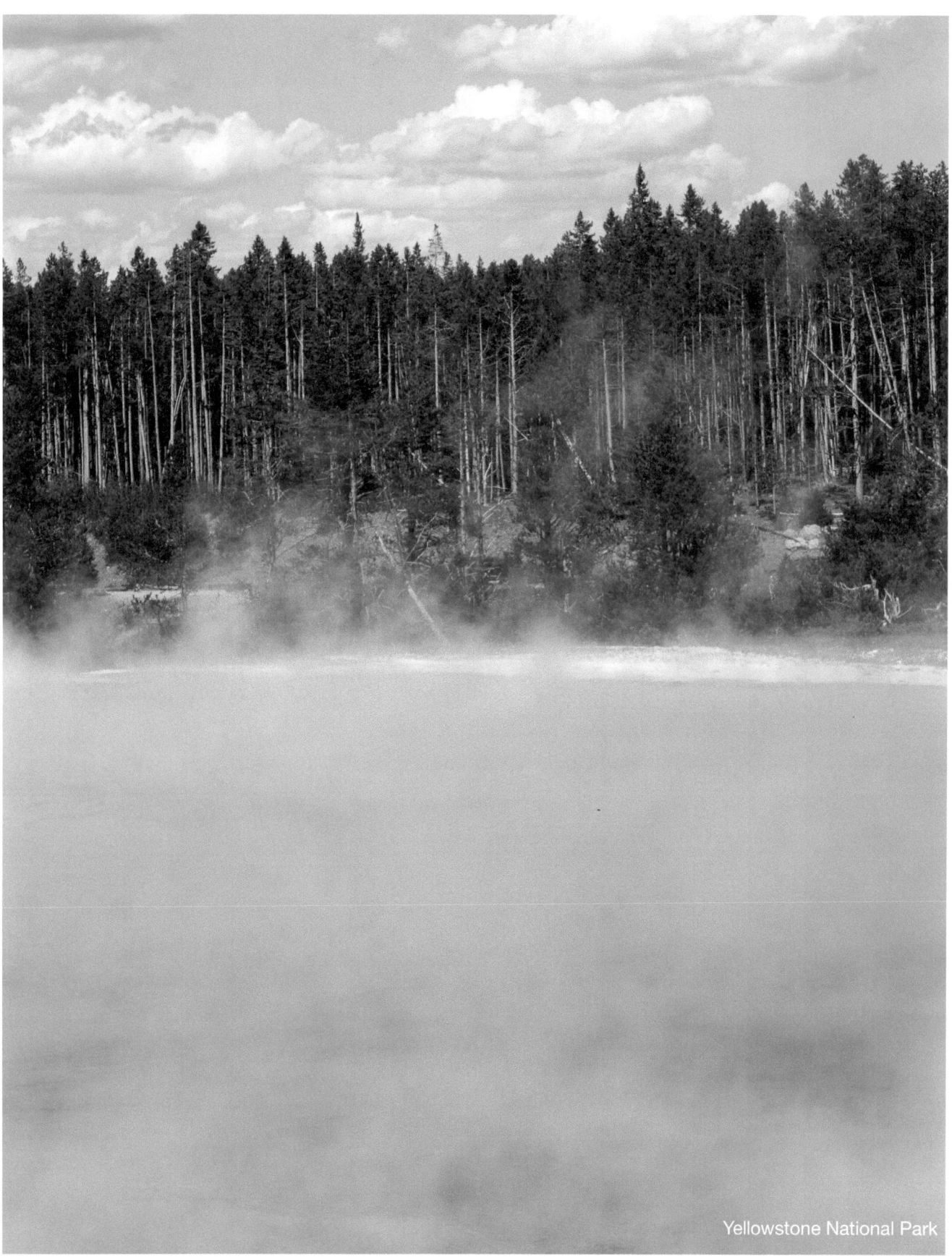

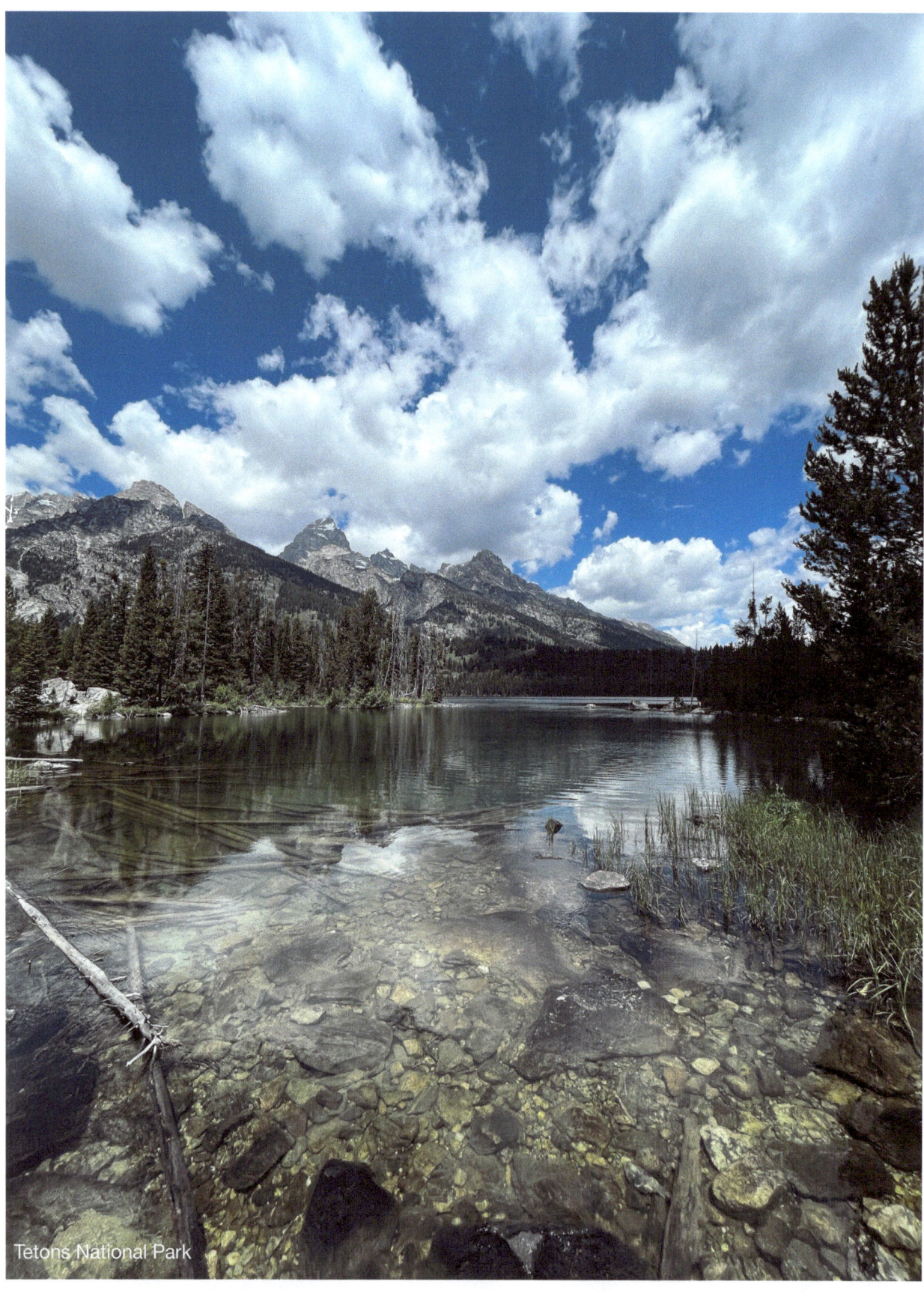

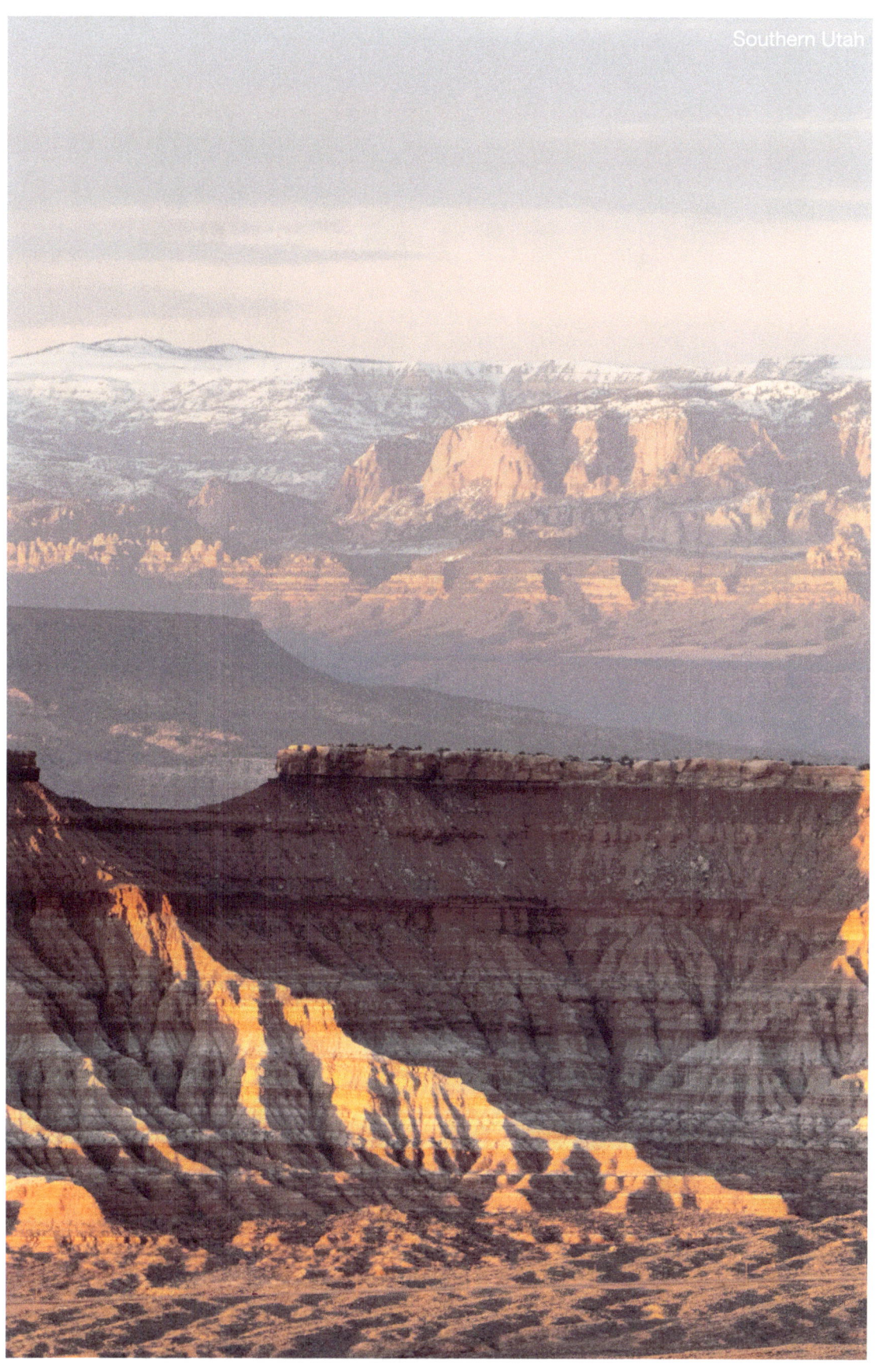
Southern Utah

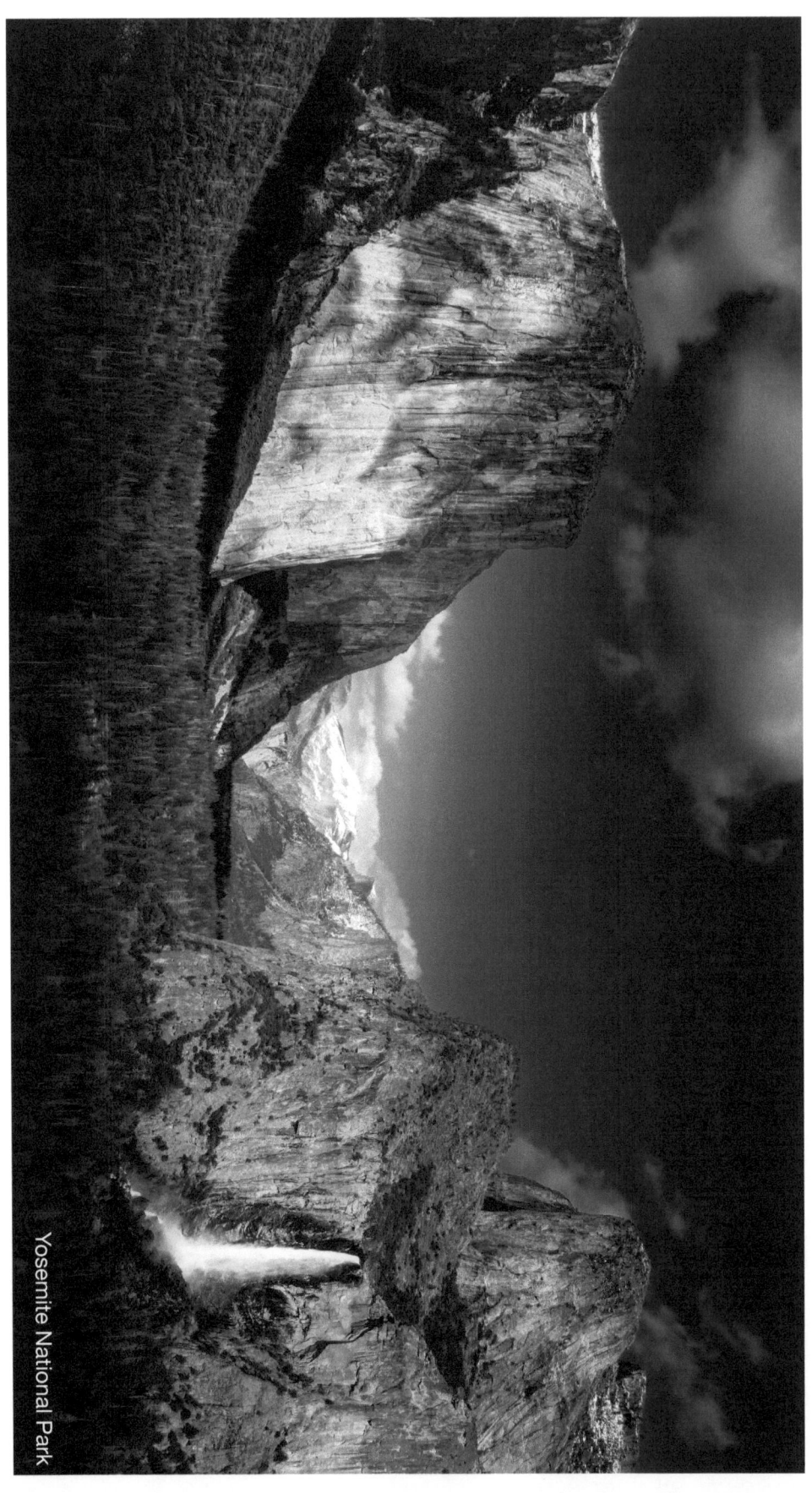
Yosemite National Park

Southern Utah

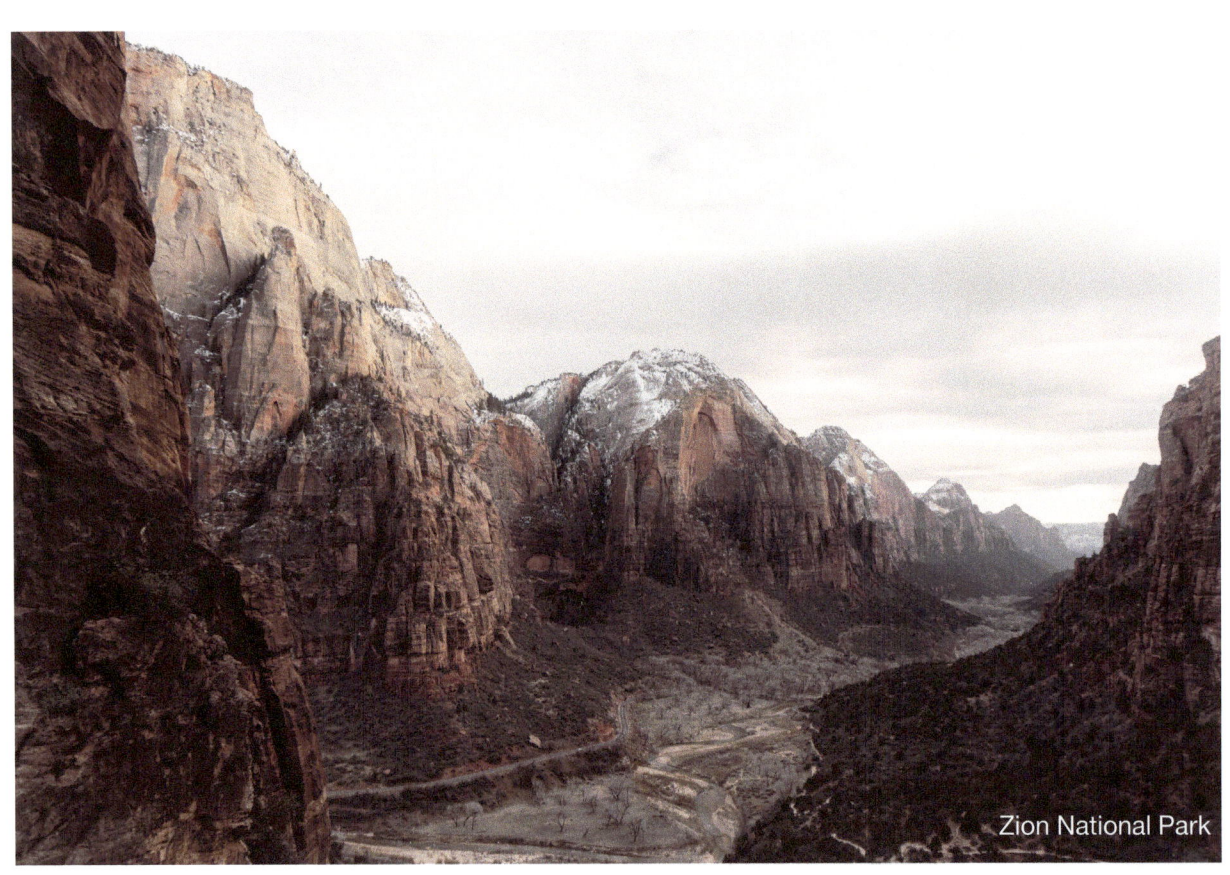

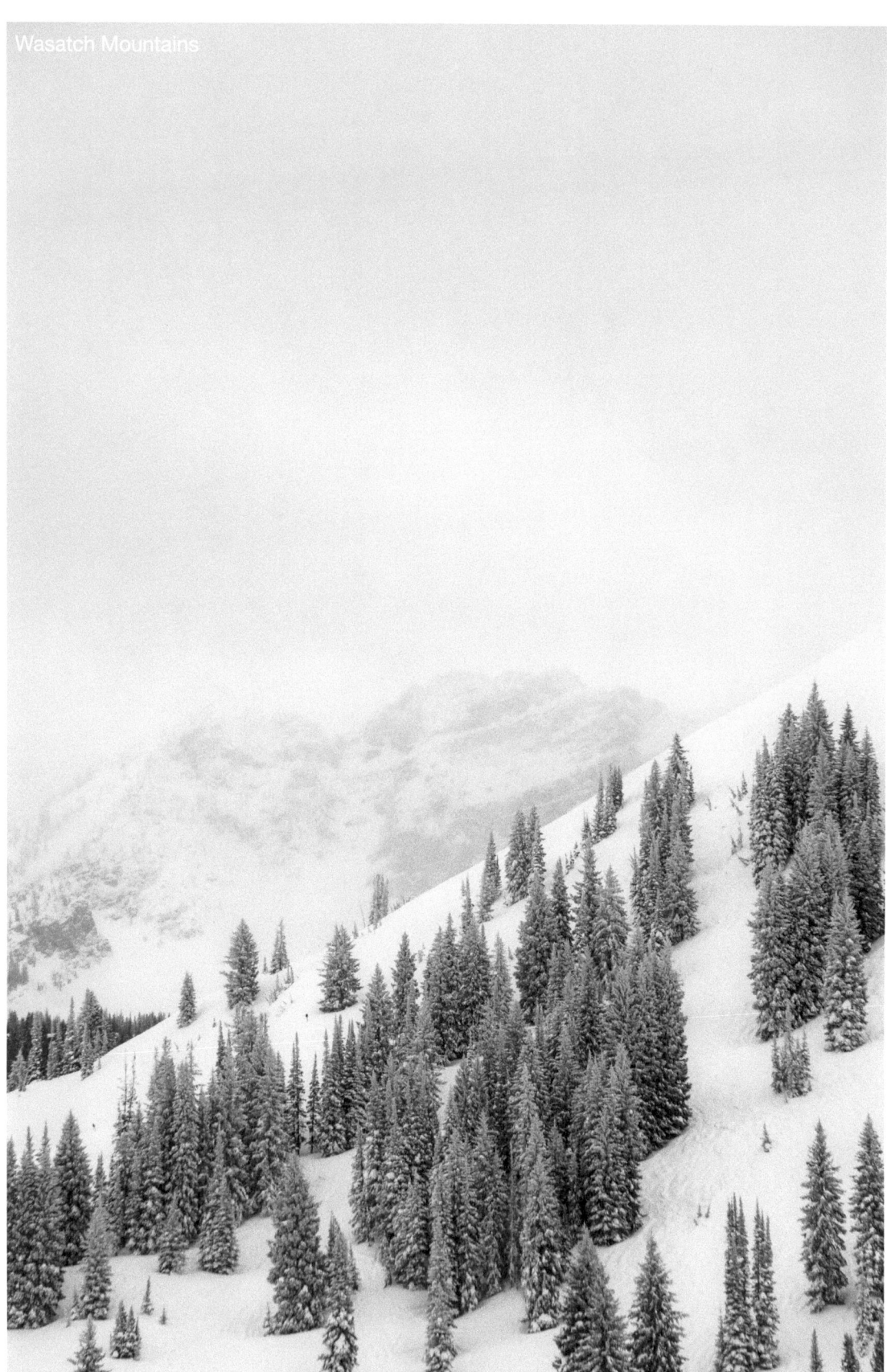

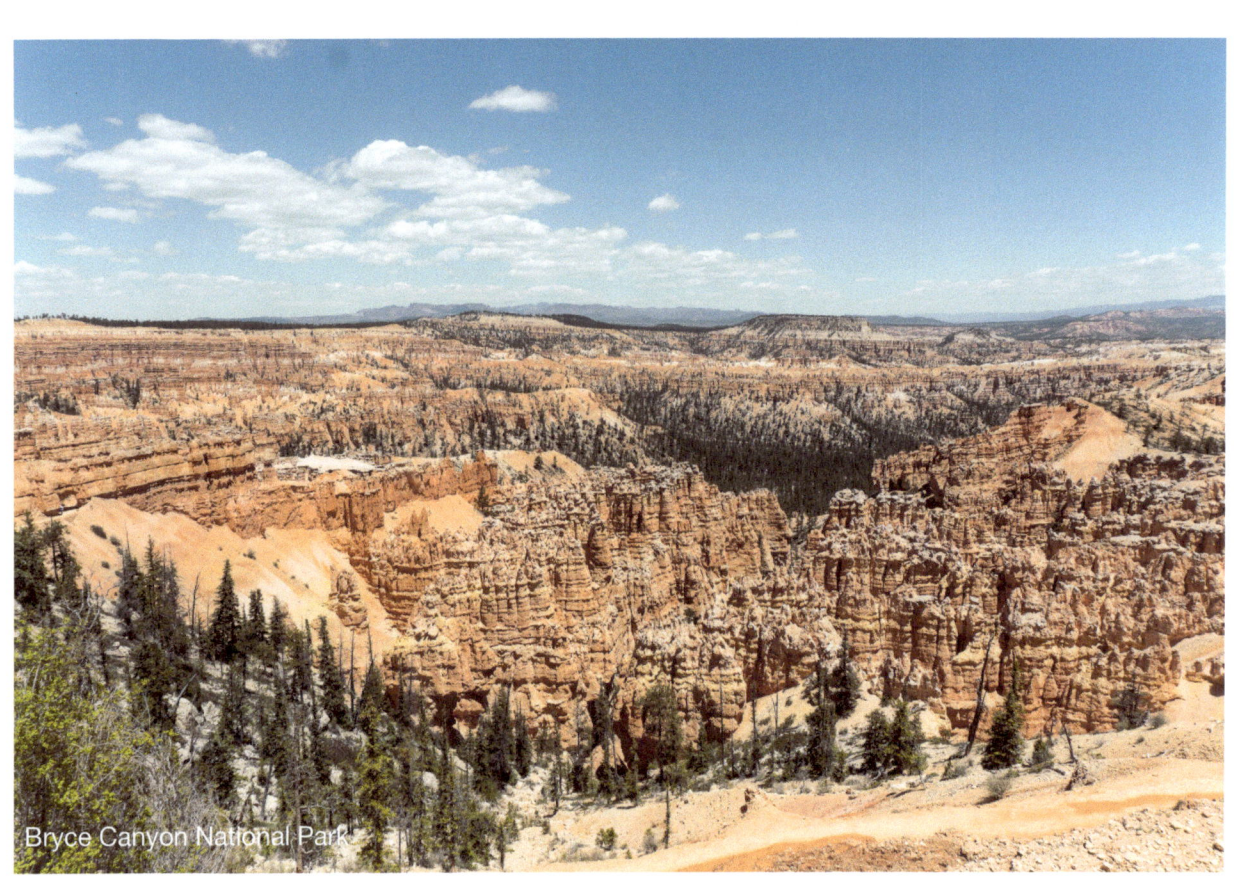

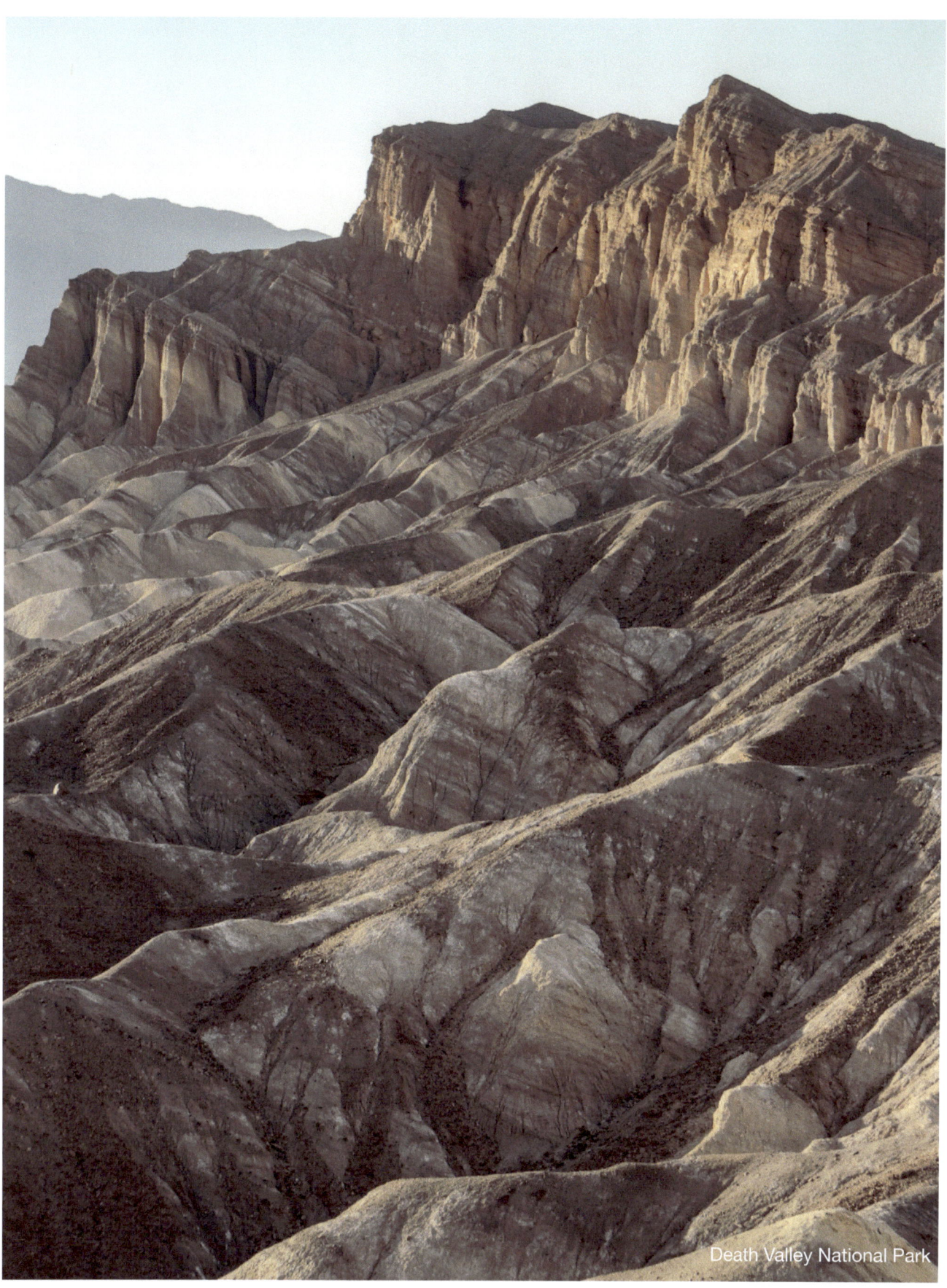

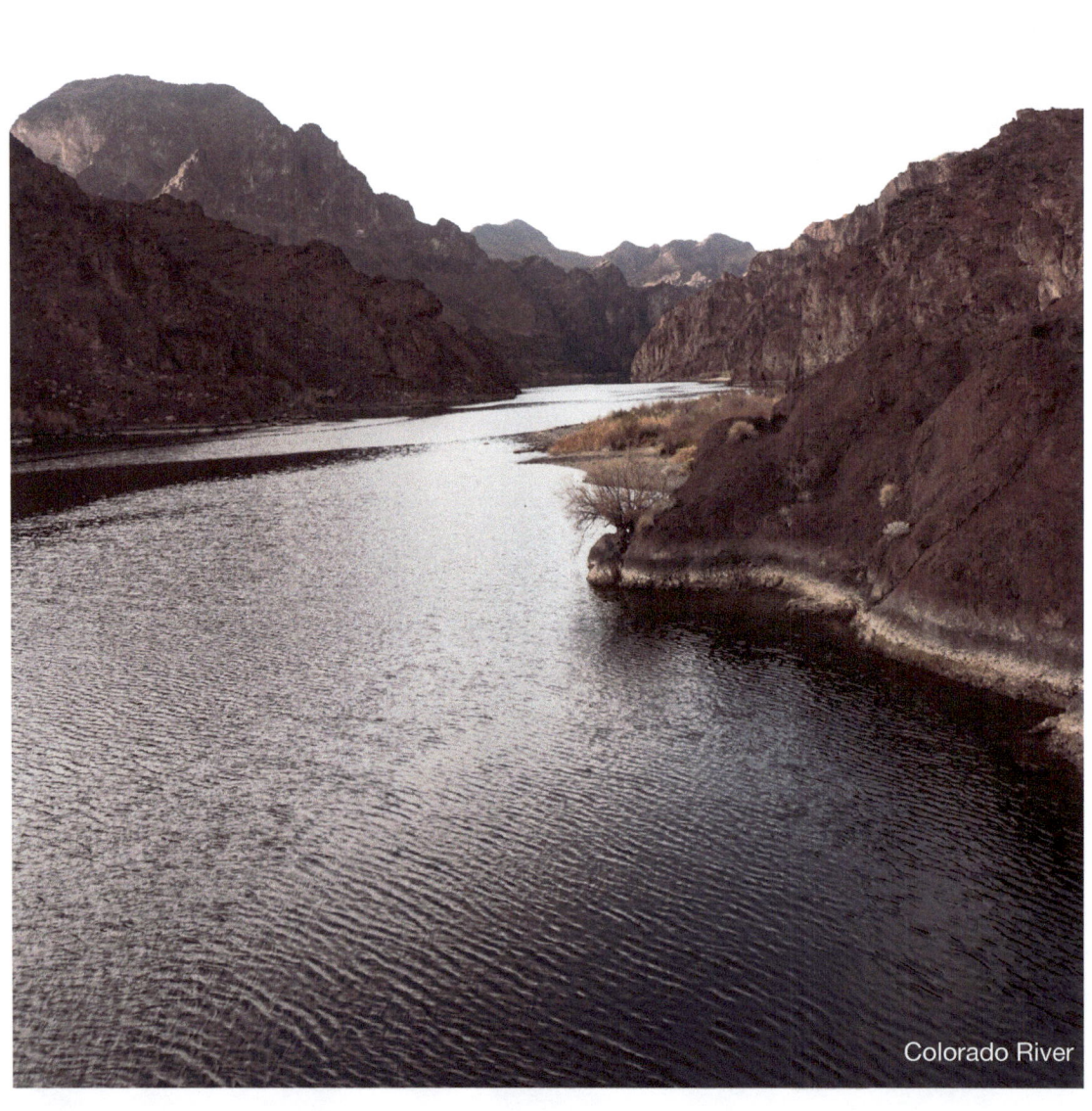

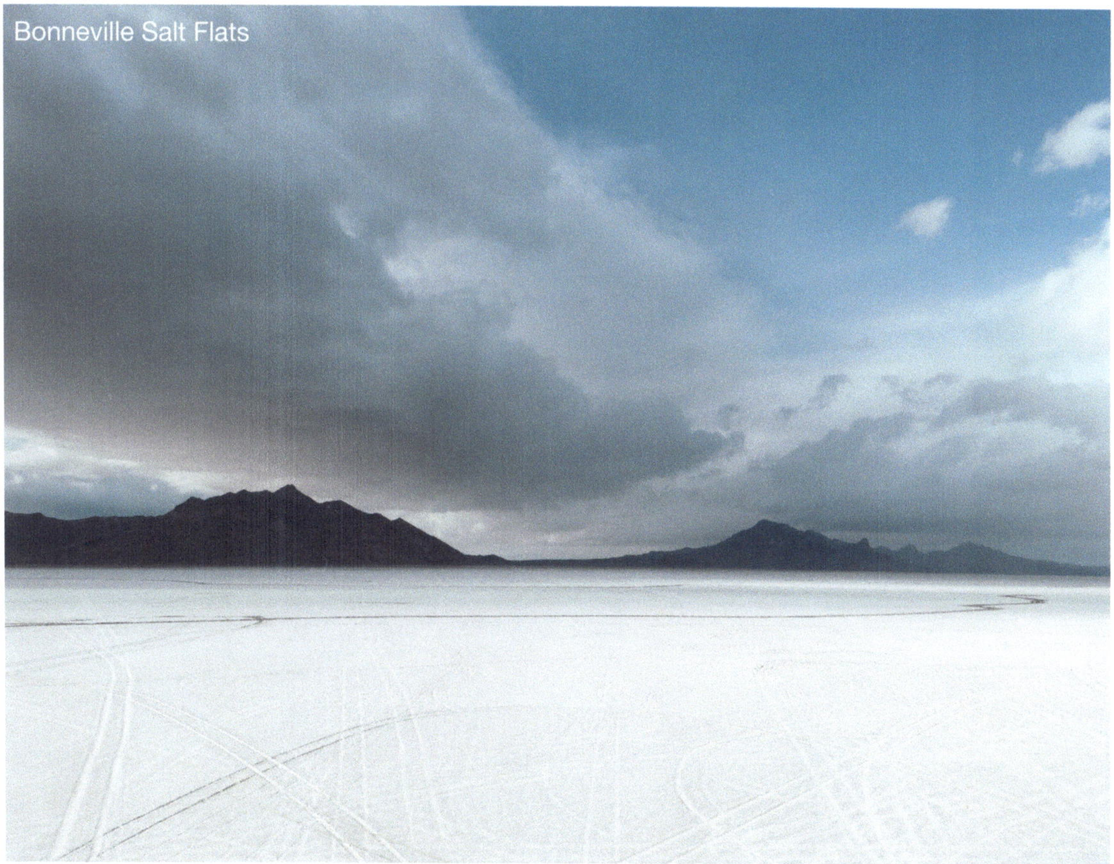

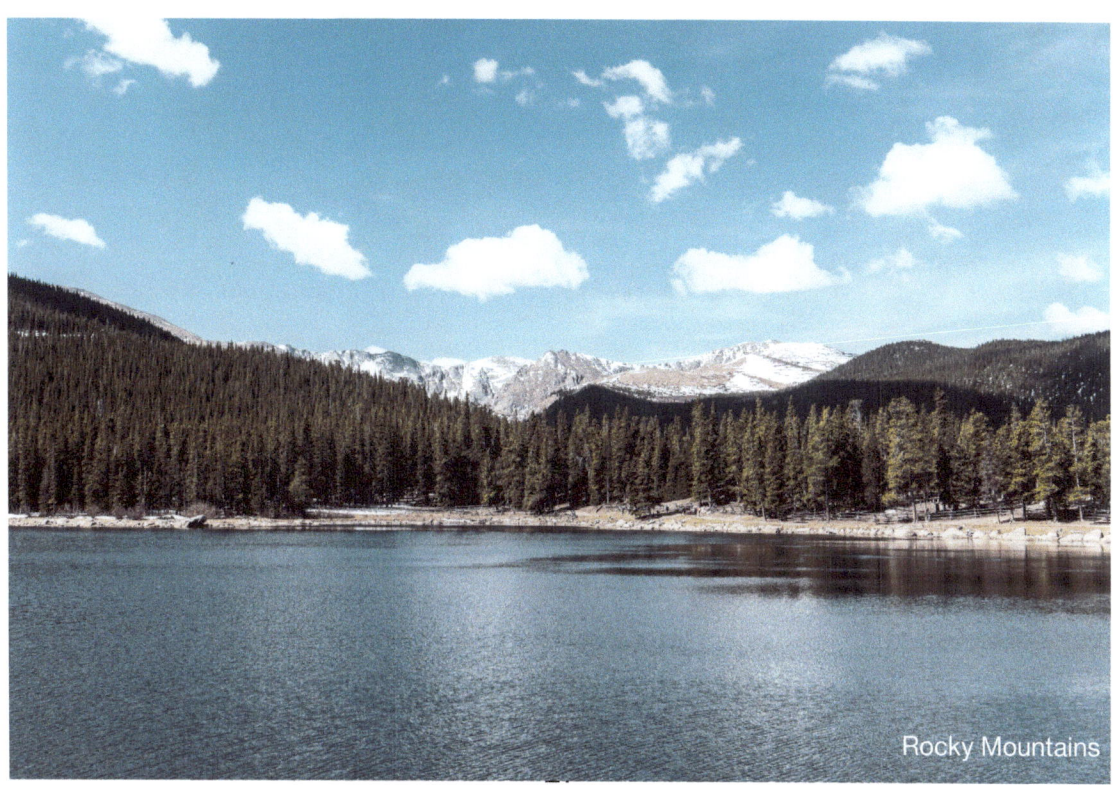

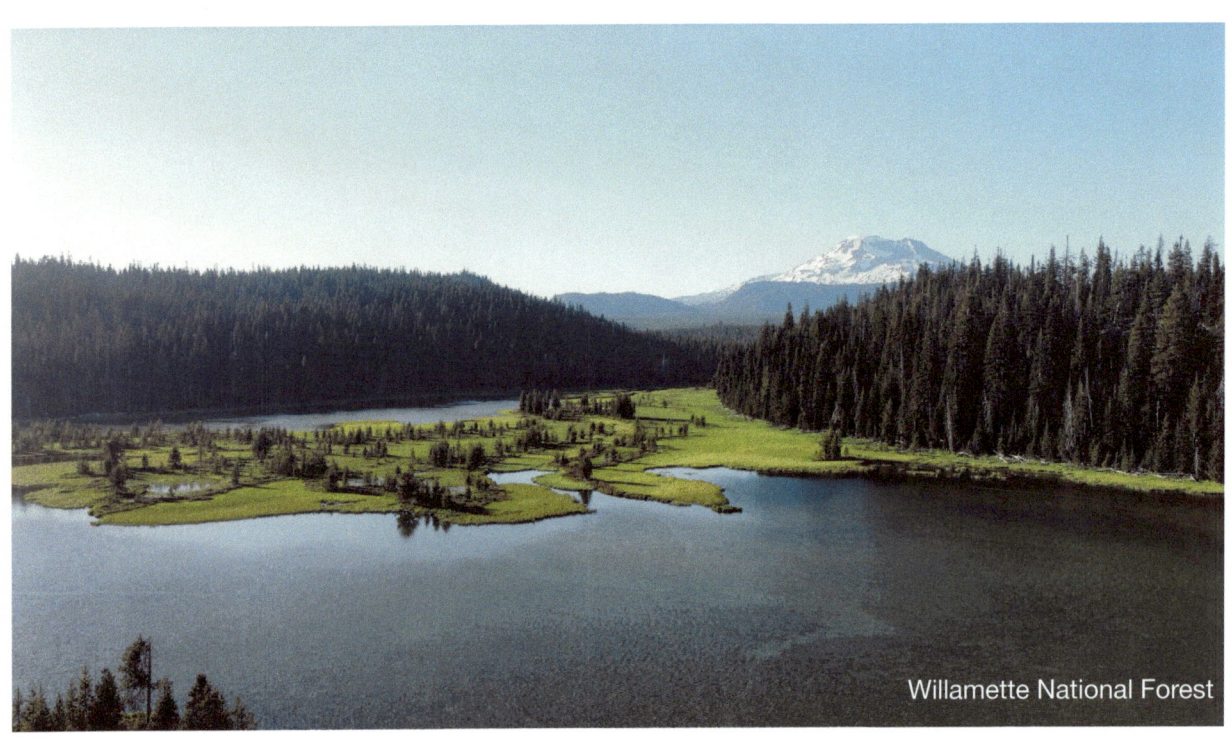
Willamette National Forest

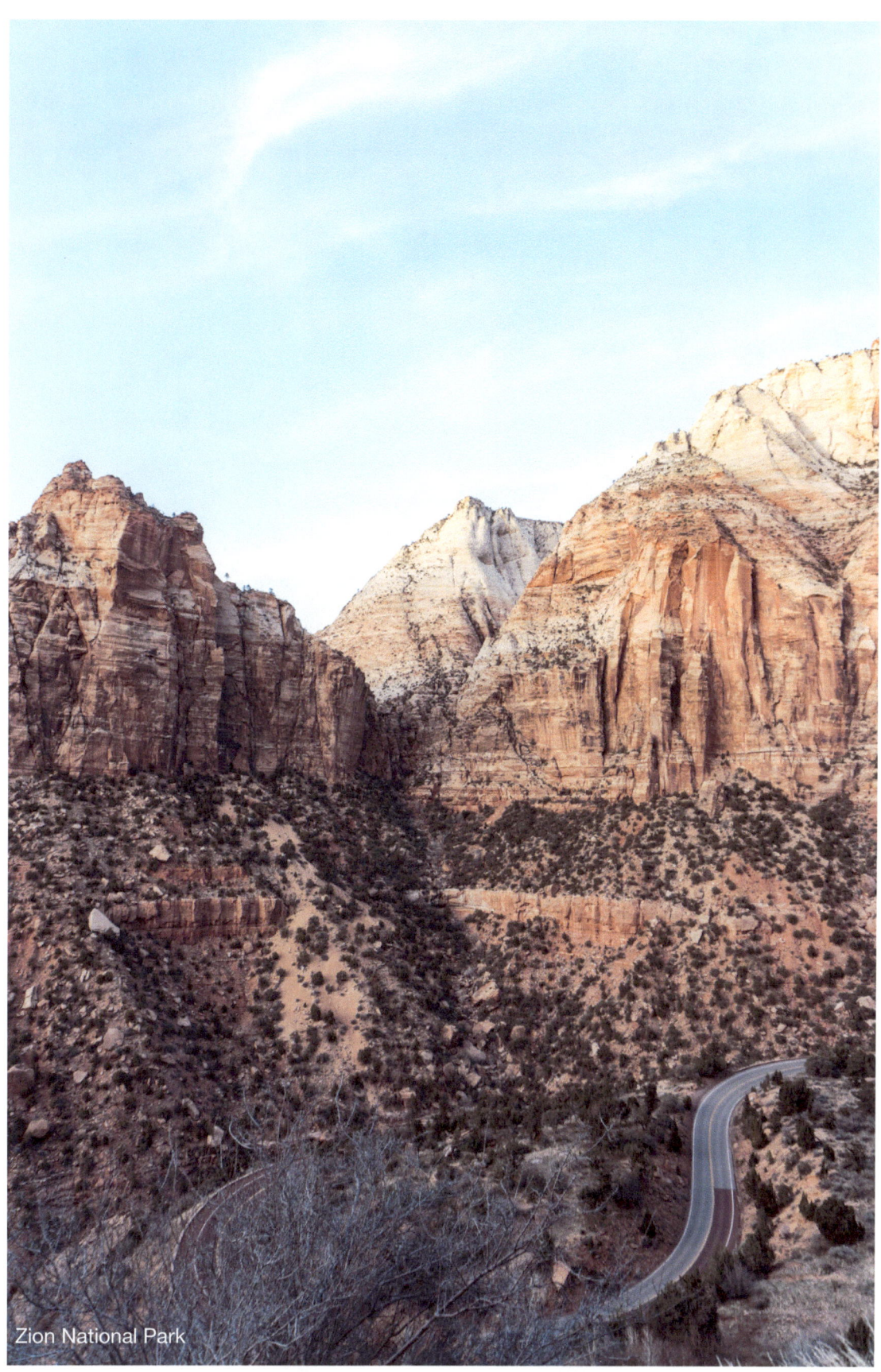

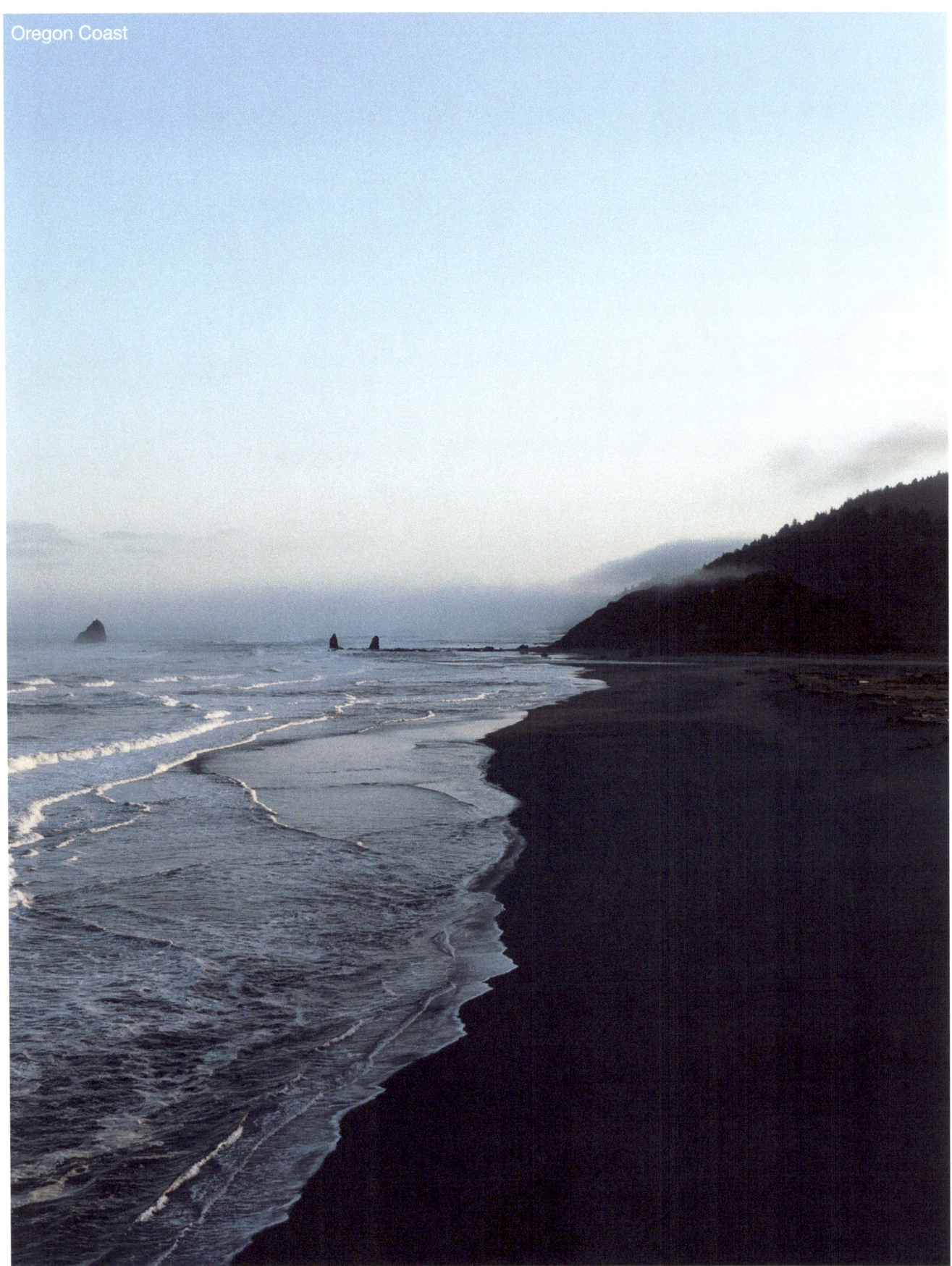
Oregon Coast

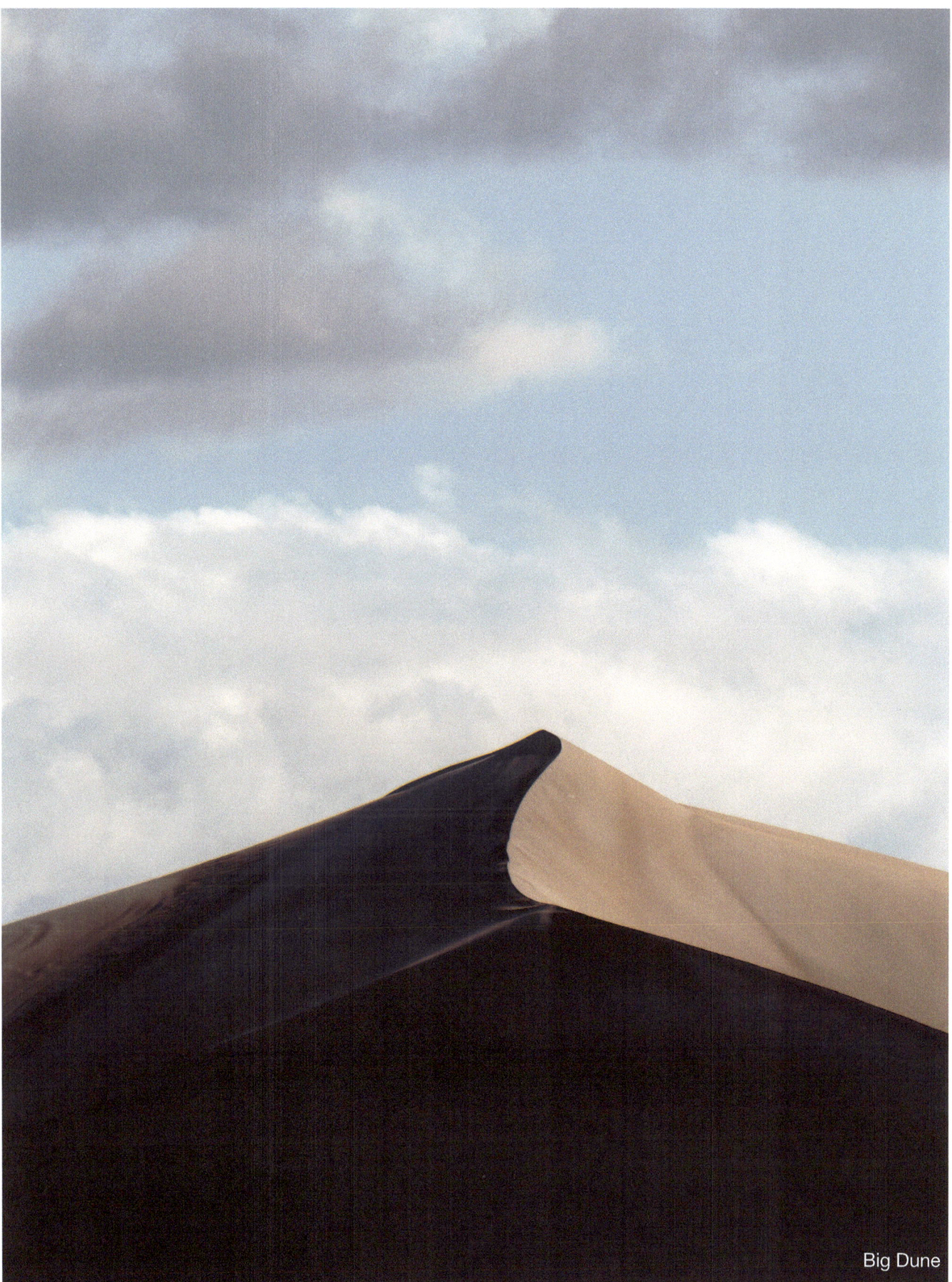
Big Dune

www.ingramcontent.com/pod-product-compliance
Lightning Source LLC
Chambersburg PA
CBHW051826210526
45473CB00005B/1755